EXPLORE the WORLD

LIFE SCIENCE

MW01280239

From Wild to Mild

ELLEN R. BRAAF

TABLE OF CONTENTS

PIONEER VALLEY EDUCATIONAL PRESS, INC

LIVING IN OUR HOUSES

Dogs have been living with humans for about 12,000 years—about twice as long as cats. In that time, dogs have changed a lot from their wolf ancestors. They have lost their killer instincts and have become cute, social, and trusting. These changes have helped them get along with humans.

But cats are a bit different. Although most cats are happy to live in our houses and eat our food, they are still a lot like their wild relatives. Behind the quiet purrs and soft fur are pointy teeth and **razor** claws. They may seem sweet, but, in many ways, they're still tigers on the inside.

So how did these tigers move into our living rooms?

CATS ARE EVERYWHERE

Lions rule the open grasslands. Tigers lurk in forests and jungles. Cougars pad over rocky slopes and through deep snowdrifts. And jaguars slosh through rivers and swamps.

All cats are hunters. They eat meat, and their bodies are built for power and speed. They walk tiptoe on their padded paws.

Their streamlined bodies, strong hearts, and large lungs help cheetahs outrun any animal on land.

Most cats are loners. But unlike dogs, cats don't care about getting along with others. They don't like following a leader or learning the rules. They like to be their own boss. They may even see other cats as **intruders**, not friends.

The lion is the rare cat that prefers to live in groups. A group of lions is called a pride.

Cats are **territorial.** This is why a meeting between two cats will often lead to a fight. They leave smell messages for each other with their urine, spit, and chemicals from scent glands on their bodies. These smells can mean different things. One says, "Keep out!" while another asks, "Looking for a mate?" A cat might also put its scent marks over another cat's marks to say, "You don't scare me."

Cats have other ways to send messages to one another. Claw marks on a tree say, "Pay attention!"

CATS FROM THE PAST

The cat's family story began about 60 million years ago with a small, tree-climbing mammal. These creatures hunted small prey with their special knifelike teeth. Over time, their teeth became more deadly. These creatures ate only meat. Their bodies lost the ability to digest plants.

These creatures lived near humans. They were **scavengers**. They raided garbage heaps and hunted mice.

The ancestor of modern house cats probably looked a lot like this small African wildcat.

A cat's jawbone from 8,000 years ago was found on an island near Greece. Because cats aren't native to this island, **archaeologists** believe that humans must have brought them there—maybe as pets.

Egyptians during that time period might have liked cats because they ate pesky rats and snakes, or maybe just because they were cute and furry. The ancient Egyptians might have left out pots of milk to encourage the helpful hunters to stay.

As years passed, the cat's importance in Egyptian culture grew. Art from that time shows cats sitting under chairs, playing, eating fish, and helping people hunt birds. Cats were even **sacred** in their religion.

Cats soon became popular pets in Egypt. When a cat died, it was buried in a special cemetery.

>> **Some Egyptian homes had cat statues to honor the cat-headed goddess Bastet.**

Soon there were cats in many places. Even though they were very helpful, people began to believe that cats were sent by the devil. People suspected them of black magic.

MORE TO EXPLORE

When their beloved cats died, some Egyptian owners **MUMMIFIED** them. They also left items for their dead pets to play with in the afterlife, as well as little bowls of milk to keep them nourished.

MICE AND RAT HUNTERS

By the Middle Ages, cats were no longer pampered pets or sacred creatures. They had to work for their food. They hunted and killed rats in cities and on farms.

Because they were so good at driving away mice, cats became popular on ships. Cats sailed on ships traveling around the world. They left kittens behind everywhere they went.

By the 1800s, cats were being bred for their fur types, colors, and sizes. Cats today are prized for their looks, not their mousing skills.

MORE TO EXPLORE

Kittens need to be handled by humans when they are very young. If they aren't, they can **BECOME WILD** and difficult to tame.

Does this mean that we've tamed the fierce hunters into purring balls of love? Maybe not. Wildness lurks just under the surface of even the tamest cats.

Wild, or **feral**, cats can still be found all over the world. They live in alleys, on farms, and around seaports. Feral cats can be a big problem. They spread diseases to animals and humans. They hunt wildlife and crowd out other native cats.

The number one cause of death among songbirds is hunting by cats.

Today, there are millions of domestic cats. They are the most popular pets in the world.

What's the secret of their success? How did they charm us? Is it because they're smart, independent, and powerful? Or because they're sleek, graceful, and soothing? Or do we find them so fascinating because they are both beauty and beast, both wild and mild, at the same time?

STRANGE MEOWS

Humans are pretty bad at reading cat body language. Cats have learned to call us with the noise that kittens make to get the attention of their mothers—meeeow.

UURRRRRRRR

Cats don't roar like lions and tigers, but they do make a variety of noises from a scary hiss to a friendly purr.

MEEOWWWWWW!!

Scientists think that cats and their owners develop their own language of meows. One tone might mean "Feed me," while another might mean "Let me out." Some pleading meows have a whiny note that mimics a human baby's cry. But unlike cat body language, the meaning of these special meows isn't the same for every cat. Cats learn which meows get results from their own particular humans.

GLOSSARY

archaeologists
scientists who study the bones
and tools of ancient people

feral
wild, not tame

intruders
creatures that go to a place
where they are not welcome

razor
a tool that cuts hair with its sharp edge

sacred
highly valued and important

scavengers
animals that search for
animal flesh to eat

territorial
keeping others out of one's area

INDEX